D'Souza's Delusion
by Paul Covell
Copyright 2012 Paul Covell

Other Books by Paul Covell
G.O.P. War On U.S. at Smashwords e-tailers & pocketbook at createspace.com/3955908
The Hail Mary, at Smashwords e-tailers & pocketbook at createspace.com/3989582
More copies of D'Souza's Delusion at Smashwords e-tailers & createspace.com/4010070

Table of Contents

"What if Obama is so outside our comprehension that only if you understand Kenyan, anti-colonial behavior, can you piece together Obama's actions? That is the most accurate, predictive model for his behavior."

Newt Gingrich, *National Review* Online.

Preface

Motivation for writing this book is not merely Dinesh D'Souza's delusion. The world could survive by ignoring D'Souza. Danger arises, however, when guileful political leaders fall prey to D'Souza's pipedreams. Former Speaker of the House Newt Gingrich seems entranced by the reverie D'Souza entertained on the genesis Barack Obama's policies. One source of Gingrich's fallacy appears to be the *Roots of Obama's Rage*. It seems that Gingrich is convinced of D'Souza's delusion that Obama's political decisions are the product of Obama's *Kenyan anti-colonialism*—an elastic concept that can take whatever form the immediate phantasm requires.

Pardon us for suggesting an equally ludicrous hypothesis. Maybe Barack Obama is under the gravitational pull of the moon? Before dismissing the possibility that the *Patient Protection And Affordable Care Act* resulted from the lunar orbit, and not Kenyan anti-colonialism, we should at least look at the East African influence, if any, on our President's policies.

Analysis of the *bona fides* of D'Souza and Gingrich leaves lingering doubts about the legitimacy of their purposes. Folks might excuse Gingrich for saying almost anything because *the man is*

2

running for president. When he is not running, Newt merely wants to be relevant in some sort of political way to the Republican who would be president. When Gingrich gets caught saying something outrageous or verifiably false, he backs away with the excuse, 'Gee, I'm just a nearly 70-year old grandfather (looking for forgiveness)'.

It is not for one writer to judge another as delusional. Nor does D'Souza appear to be clinically impaired. The problem is that the words D'Souza writes frequently appear to be the product of a hallucination. In looking at D'Souza's theories, one suspects that even D'Souza does not believe the nonsense he spouts.

To see the scope of the peril facing the Nation on the political front, we must view D'Souza's contributions as a few distorted chips in a larger mosaic of dishonesty by the greater G.O.P. entourage that is assaulting the electorate with the *Big Lie*. In evaluating pundits and politicians, there is an adage as old as the history of finance. "*Follow the money*".

Oligarchs and plutocrats doubtless want to hold onto their wealth. Warren Buffet's donation of more than $30 billion to the *Bill And Malinda Gates Foundation* is the exception rather than the rule. Charles Koch, David Koch and Sheldon Adelson and their associates contributed upwards of $400 million to Republicans in the 2012 Presidential and Congressional Campaign, to make sure that "*government of the people, by the people, for the people*", if it does not perish under a flood of political propaganda ads, will at a minimum not result in a tax increase aimed at the upper two percent.

There are two major methods of enjoying wealth. One is to make money yourself, buy the toys that delight and invest the balance in enduring resources. For Dinesh D'Souza and Paul Ryan, and Republicans in general, the goal is to protect rich people from poor people taking away the wealth of rich people. The latter preoccupation results in battalions of pundits rallying around a materialistic and sterile cause called *"Conservatism"*. Of course, there are patriotic slogans and references to liberty, free enterprise and the entrepreneurial spirit thrown into the mix for rallying effect. The bottom line, however, is money and what money can buy. The gloss of liberty and First Amendment freedoms is a thin veneer adorned with flags.

What is sad is that Conservatives act as though it is necessary to defame Progressives in order to safeguard the money of the Oligarchs. Thus was born the profane crusade to delegitimize President Barack Obama. After surviving four bankruptcies, Donald Trump managed to retain enough wealth to qualify as the drum major of the *"birther"* brigade—those who claim the President is not one of us or even born in the U.S.

Republican *"Talking Points"* are like chaff in the wind. The Republican National Committee and Republican Campaign Committee feed the propaganda to their robotic candidate. Mitt

Romney tells us that Barack Obama is "foreign". John H. Sununu gives affirmation by wishing Obama "would learn to be an American". Sununu could never be President, having been born in Havana, Cuba, to a Lebanese mother and a Palestinian father. How American is that! Or, maybe D'Souza, Romney and Sununu are right, and the roots of the *Affordable Care Act* did originate in Nairobi?

At the end of the day, Republicans who continually smear our President should apologize. Not to Barack Obama. The President can weather the storm. The defamers should apologize to the Nation, which the *Big Lie* tarnished.

The more Republicans unleash the *Big Lie* to try to disqualify President Obama, the more the Electorate disbelieves Republican propaganda. It is obvious who the enemy is. Republicans want to destroy public education by giving vouchers to those who have no need. Republicans want to destroy Medicare by giving undervalue vouchers to Seniors. Republicans want to privatize Social Security so Wall Street can make a fast buck. Republican leaders represent the one percent. Newt Gingrich is so desperate to be relevant to something that he campaigns in Missouri for Reprehensible Todd Akin, the man who believes that "legitimate" rape cannot cause pregnancy.

***

"For the love of money is the root of all evil."
1 Timothy 6:10.

Chapter -1-

Follow the Money.

If there is a quick buck to be made, Republicans will propose to destroy democratic institutions to allow entrepreneurs to make money. The United States has a proud history of public education. Boston Latin School, founded in 1635, is the oldest continuous public school in the Nation. Every State in the Union provides public education to all inhabitants, without regard to race, creed, income level, and in many cases even nationality. Governor Jan Brewer (R-AZ), however, is asking for, '*Papers, Please*'. Jeb Bush and his Republican allies want to gut public education by giving vouchers to parents of students in private schools.

The result will be the destruction of the public school system. Funds will be diverted from public schools to pay for vouchers that are tickets out of the public school system. At first, it will be a trickle of money leaving public schools. As public schools are weakened by loss of funding, the trickle of diverted money will become a flood as more parents seek to flee public education. George Romney chose to place Mitt Romney in Cranbrook, an exclusive private prep school in Bloomfield Hills, Michigan.

If school vouchers were available in the 1960s, George Romney could have received public funds to pay for part of the cost of Mitt Romney's private education. Multiply this loss of money to public schools today by millions of private students, and the result to public education would be devastating. Jeb Bush cannot wait until he can install vouchers to kill public education. Jeb Bush's concoction of lethal *Flavor Aid* will be camouflaged as giving parents a choice.

Republicans want to give Seniors a voucher that will not have sufficient value to pay for health insurance. Mitt Romney picked Paul Ryan for Vice President. Ryan is the Chair of the Budget Committee in the House of Reprehensibles. Ryan wrote the Republican Budget, called the *Path to Prosperity*. Ryan plans to replace Medicare with a voucher system that will leave Seniors at the mercy of health insurers.

For the past thirty years, Republicans planned to privatize Social Security so their friends on Wall Street can make a profit. In 2012, however, the Electorate understands what the Republicans intend to do with democratic institutions that protect the People from the one percent. Even $800 million in Republican propaganda cannot hide the truth.

McCain Feingold

John McCain (R-AZ) operates on three tracks. One is the conservative Republican warrior, who wants to see the U.S. do something more aggressive in Syria and Iran, and stand up to China and Russia. The second McCain is the caring maverick, who wants to make America a better place. The third is the fighter pilot, who instinctively flies by the seat of his pants. The maverick does the most good. McCain and former Senator Russ Feingold (R-WI) saw that political campaign contributions posed a threat of corruption to the body politic. *McCain Feingold Act of 2002* set limits on campaign contributions under the supervision of the Federal Election Commission.

As an inveterate watchdog for the plutocrats, Senator Mitch McConnell (R-KY) immediately filed suit as *plaintiff* to protect the First Amendment rights of the rich to speak their minds and spend their pocketbooks in support of unlimited free speech. The Supreme Court decision in *McConnell v Federal Election Commission ("FEC")* (2003) 540 U.S. 93, comprised nearly as many separate opinions as there were Justices. The decision in *McConnell* was indecipherable, and had paragraphs and even footnotes that would choke a horse. It was only a matter of time until the *Bipartisan Campaign Reform Act* would collapse from perceived incompatibility with the broad sweep of the First Amendment.

Hillary: The Movie brought the house down. In January 2008, the movie smeared the Democratic candidate through interviews with such conservative notables as Dick Morris and Ann Coulter, rehashing the nonsense dredged up by the seven-year Independent Counsel investigation of the *Whitewater* land investment that the Clintons made in Arkansas in the 1980s. The U.S. Government blocked broadcast of the film on cable TV just before the start of the Democratic primaries. In *Citizens United v. FEC* (2010) 558 U.S. 50, Chief Justice John Roberts and four other conservatives held unconstitutional most of *McCain Feingold's* limitations on political speech. Corporations could spend as much as they wanted to on political campaigns.

The presidency, the Congress and the entire of apparatus of state and federal governments are for sale to the highest bidder. Contributors to campaigns could remain anonymous if they contributed to independent Political Action Committees (PACs) rather than directly to a candidate's campaign. Senator McConnell was delighted. The mega wealthy could own the Nation without any limitation imposed by law. Senator Bernie Sanders (I-VT) was aghast, and called for a constitutional amendment to control campaign contributions.

Mitt Romney, the Republican candidate for president seemed to take *Citizens* in stride. During the 2012 campaign, Romney famously remarked, *"Corporations are people my friend"*. Republicans were overjoyed at their newly protected First Amendment rights of free speech and freedom to associate and promote the ideas and candidacies of whomever they assumed would govern the *"right way"*.

Sheldon Adelson, owner of casinos in Las Vegas and Macao, thought there was still some mileage left in New Gingrich, and contributed $5 million to Gingrich's 2012 primary run. When that money ran out, Miriam Adelson donated another $5 million to Gingrich. When the Gingrich campaign collapsed after a barrage of negative advertising unleashed by Mitt Romney, the Adelsons pledged another $100 million for freedom, free enterprise and a patriotic government that would not include Barack Obama as President and Eric Holder as Attorney General.

Managing a large amount of the *House Money* directed against President Obama is the nimble gambler, Karl Rove, formerly known as *Bush's Brain*. In 2003, George W. Bush claimed in his State of the Union Speech that Saddam Hussein obtained yellow cake uranium from Niger. Former Ambassador Joe Wilson went to Africa for the CIA to investigate. Wilson debunked the Bush claim in a New York Times Op-Ed, "*What I Didn't Find In Africa*". Dick Cheney was outraged at Wilson's undermining of Bush's Weapons of Mass Destruction (WMD) justification for invading Iraq.

Cheney decided to sic the dogs on Wilson and his wife, Valerie Plame, who was a covert agent for the CIA. Cheney's lame theory was, '*Maybe Wilson's wife sent him to Africa*'. At the time, Karl Rove was Deputy Chief of Staff for President Bush, and Irwin ("Scooter") Libby was Chief of Staff for Cheney. The attack dogs gambled that they could discredit Wilson's debunking of WMD, expose the status of a covert CIA Agent to the media and get away with it—despite a federal law prohibiting disclosure of the identity of a covert intelligence agent.

U.S. Attorney Patrick Fitzgerald convened a Grand Jury to investigate possible violation of federal law. Scooter Libby incriminated himself by lying about his involvement, was indicted, tried and convicted. Karl Rove appeared before the Grand Jury *five times*. Rove's gamble paid off. Neither Rove, nor Cheney as ringleader, was indicted. Cheney demanded that Bush pardon Scooter Libby. Bush refused a pardon, but commuted Libby's prison sentence.

As the result of slick footwork before the Grand Jury in the *Valerie Plame Affair*, Karl Rove today is managing distribution to "*conservative*" candidates of hundreds of millions of dollars through his Super PACs (Political Action Committees), *American Crossroads* and *Crossroads GPS*. Karl Rove's goal is to promote freedom, free enterprise and a patriotic government that does not include Barack Obama as President or Eric Holder as Attorney General.

"Not long ago, Karl Rove seemed toxic: the brains of a disastrous presidency, tarred by scandal. Today, as the mastermind of a billion-dollar war chest—and with surrogates in place in the Romney campaign—he's the de facto leader of the Republican Party. But in Rove's long game, 2012 may just be the beginning." *Vanity Fair* online, *Letter from Washington*, September 2012.

The *Letter* notes that "Rove had an incredibly powerful ally", the U.S. Supreme Court, which confirmed Bush's election in 2000 in

Bush v. Gore, "one of the most notorious decisions in its history", and in 2010 "once again provided the answer to Karl Rove's prayers, this time in the form of *Citizens United v. Federal Election Commission*".

Charles and David Koch (collectively, the "Koch Brothers") own and manage Koch Industries, Inc., an industrial conglomerate that is the second largest privately held company in the U.S. *Americans For Prosperity, LLC,* is a tax-exempt propaganda front for the Koch Brothers. Herman Cain, former head of *Godfather's Pizza*, was a motivational speaker for *Americans For Prosperity*.

The Koch Brothers entered Herman Cain in the 2012 Republican Primary, as if it were a beauty contest that could be manipulated by the right amount of propaganda. Cain immediately went to the top of the polls as flavor of the month. When Cain's candidacy fizzled a month later, the Koch Brothers pledged $100 million, or more, to the Romney Campaign or to PACs that support Romney. The Koch Brothers are dedicated to freedom, free enterprise and a patriotic government that does not include Barack Obama as President or Eric Holder as Attorney General.

Rumor has it that Chief Justice John Roberts is concerned about the flak taken by the Supreme Court as result of *Bush v. Gore*, which happened on Chief Justice Rehnquist's watch, and *Citizen's United v. FEC*, which happened on Roberts' watch. Roberts is eager to try to take the politics out of Supreme Court decisions—a daunting task that may require Roberts occasionally to vote with the progressive wing of the Court. Roberts failed to modify or reverse *Citizens United*, however, when occasions arose to revisit campaign contributions as free speech.

The Republican Assault on the *Affordable Care Act* rose to fever pitch when the Court decided *Nat'l. Fed. Ind. Business v. Sebelius* (2012) 567 U.S. ___ . Republicans expected Chief Justice Roberts to strike down Obamacare as an unconstitutional expansion of federal power under the *Commerce Clause*. Roberts surprised with a ruling that the Act was constitutional under the federal power to tax. The decision saved Obamacare, but lent credence to the Republican *Big Lie* that the *Affordable Care Act* constituted the largest tax increase in U.S. history.

***

"He is able who thinks he is able".

Prince Gautama Siddharta.

Chapter -2-

Why Single Out Dinesh D'Souza?

With so many conservative fanatics running amok with extreme theories, why single out D'Souza for special consideration. First, D'Souza's more recent theories are especially goofy. Second, Republican leaders like former Speaker Newt Gingrich use D'Souza's fantasies to support conservative attacks on progressives. Picking up from *The Roots of Obama's Rage*, Gingrich seriously proposes that *"only if you understand Kenyan anti-colonial behavior, can you piece together Obama's actions"*. Gingrich's formulation of D'Souza's pipedream must be confusing to the people in Peoria, as they try to analyze the *Affordable Care Act* from the perspective of the President's imaginary Kenyan anti-colonialism. It is a fool's errand to try to *"piece together"* anti-Obama gibberish offered by D'Souza and Gingrich.

We have to presume that Gingrich believed the statement when he made it, and that D'Souza believed it when he wrote it. This leaves members of the public—exposed to the Kenyan anti-colonial behavior tag of the President—in a state of confusion as to Barack Obama's motivations. Add to this Romney's references to the President's ideas as *"foreign"* and Republicans' claims that Obama is a *"Socialist"*, and it would be obvious why some voters are perplexed by the Republican *Big Lie* campaign.

D'Souza came to America with good credentials. Born in Mumbai, India, on April 25, 1961, D'Souza is a few months older than Barack Obama. D'Souza took early schooling with the Jesuits at St. Stanislaus High School and completed 11th and 12th grades at Sydenham College, both in Mumbai, formerly Bombay. He also studied at Patagonia High School, Patagonia, Arizona, before earning a B.A. in English at Dartmouth College.

D'Souza was editor of *Policy Review*, a quarterly owned by the *Heritage Foundation*. He went after the Catholic Bishops for, of all things, promoting peace. According to *Wikipedia* and other sites, "In *The Bishops as Pawns*, D'Souza theorized that U.S. Catholic bishops were being manipulated by American liberals in agreeing to oppose U.S. military buildup and use of power abroad and actually knew very little about these subjects to which they were lending their credibility".

D'Souza claimed that: "interviews with these bishops suggest they know little or nothing about the ideas and proposals to which they are putting their signature and lending their religious authority. The bishops are unfamiliar with existing defense and economic programs, unable to identify even in general terms the Soviet military capability, ignorant of roughly how much of the budget currently goes to defense, unclear of how much should be reallocated to social programs, and innocent of the most basic concepts underlying the intelligent layman's discussion of these questions". Thus spake D'Souza.

President Barack Obama doubtless does not feel that the Catholic bishops are a pushover for the government today, after they sued to stop distribution of contraceptives to employees of catholic schools, hospitals and charities.

In putting down the American bishops, D'Souza set himself up as an expert in Economics and Defense Policy, proving the adage that an expert is anyone more than one thousand miles from home.

D'Souza went on to work as an advisor in the Reagan White House, before joining the *American Enterprise Institute* and the *Hoover Institution*. In 2010, D'Souza became president of Kings College in New York, N.Y.

When asked by some immigrants from Asia, '*When do I know I am an American*', D'Souza responded, '*When you vote Republican*'. In other words, Democrats and their supporters are second-class citizens. The in-crowd is Republican. As a self-conscious immigrant, D'Souza fled to the Republican intellectual ghetto in a futile attempt to become "*All-American*". Given the sorry state of the G.O.P. as one-dimensional guardians of the wealth and privileges of the Koch Brothers and Sheldon Adelson, D'Souza's descent to delusion is pathetic to observe as he holds out his tin cup for a tuppence from his masters.

In September 2010, D'Souza wrote an article in *Forbes* Magazine, *How Obama Thinks*. According to D'Souza, "our President is trapped in his father's time machine. Incredibly, the U.S. is being ruled according to the dreams of a *Luo* tribesman of the 1950s. This philandering, inebriated African socialist, who raged against the world for denying him the realization of his anticolonial ambitions, is now setting the nation's agenda through the reincarnation of his dreams in his son. The son makes it happen, but he candidly admits he is only living his father's dream. The invisible father provides the inspiration, and the son dutifully gets the job done. America today is governed by a ghost." Thus spake D'Souza.

For more of D'Souza's rubbish, one could dredge up *The Roots of Obama's Rage*. If you are waiting for the movie, it is entitled *2016*. (Where will you be in 2016, if Obama is re-elected in 2012?) The reason D'Souza stayed in America is that people in India would not pay a penny to read or see any of D'Souza's delusion. The reason America bestows wealth on far right political fantasists is that there is a cratering conservative movement that will pay any price for brickbats to lever President Obama or any other progressive out of office.

One of the themes of *2016,* to give viewers a better understanding of Barack Obama, is that, '*Love him, or hate him, you don't know him*'. Who more deserves that caution than D'Souza, who does not know what he is talking about. D'Souza takes his cue from the Romney campaign, which refused to be restricted by fact checkers or by facts.

D'Souza mischaracterized the President's father. Visualizing the President's father at the University of Hawaii, the image of the *Luo* tribesman does not come to mind. Whatever the failings or political persuasion of the father, neither can be attributed to the son. The *irrefutable proof* D'Souza offers that the son "*candidly admits he is*

17

only living his father's dream" is the title of the son's book. *Dreams From My Father.* If the President were not under the influence of Kenyan anti-colonialism, D'Souza reasons seriously that the son's book would bear the title, *Dreams Of My Father.* Dinesh has a low threshold for proof of his cockamamie theories.

As D'Souza bankrolls money from his delusion, he must marvel at the gullibility of the American audiences who pay for his twaddle. D'Souza would be laughed out of any self-respecting town in India. Maharajas do not employ servants to write polemics.

D'Souza's latest book is *Obama's America: Unmaking the American Dream,* released in 2012 by *Regnery* Publishing. *Obama's America* is a continuation of the delusion that *"Obama is hell-bent on seeing America fail".* *Regnery's* rationale is that *"Obama is applying his anti-colonial ideology to unmake America and turn it into a country our Founders would not recognize".* Neither D'Souza nor *Regnery* gives a cogent explanation of how Kenyan anti-colonialism manifests itself in the President's policies. *Regnery* is to publishing as *Fox News* is to broadcasting.

Building castles in the air, D'Souza uses ethereal materials. Most observers conclude that the President's father played virtually no role in the son's development. Master psychologist D'Souza has a contrary explanation. The son's life was an abyss because of the absence of the father. The son, therefore, determined to live the father's life as a way of fulfilling the son's life. The result is that "America today is ruled by a ghost".

President Obama did not have much exposure to Kenyan anti-colonialism at Occidental College or at Columbia or Harvard. There were two brief trips to Kenya. Maybe Kenya requires a short course on anti-colonialism at the airport for entry. At all events, it must be difficult for President Obama to fit disparate policies such as health care and the reduction of al Qaeda fighters into a Kenyan anti-colonial regime. Nor is it at all clear how Kenyan anti-colonialism would match with other policies of the U.S government.

Since there is no evidence of Kenyan anti-colonialism motivating any of Obama's policies, it serves no purpose to try to analyze D'Souza's Delusion as it relates to the President's agenda on a policy by policy basis. Suffice it to say that conservatives want to limit Barack Obama to one term in office, presumably to prevent an increase in taxes on the upper two percent.

***

"President Obama has a tendency not to be truthful."
Mitt Romney, 9/14/12, setting the scene for Romney-Ryan fibbing on a grand scale.

Chapter -3-

Intellectual Dishonesty

Mitt Romney set the course for the presidential debates and the balance of the campaign. Truth is the first casualty of war. Romney saw John McCain take the high road in 2008—and lose. Romney has no intention of going down without a no-holds-barred fight. Romney will use every slur, divisive social issue, deception and the *Big Lie* to win. By accusing the President of not being truthful, Romney signaled Romney's intent to rely on the *Big Lie*.

Republicans advance a debate in 2012 that is the opposite of what they believe. As Romney and Ryan career from deceptive response to misleading factoid, like billiard balls randomly bouncing against the rails and going off in unexpected directions, it becomes painfully apparent that their campaign is a subterfuge. After surviving a primary by placating the base, most politicians run to the center. Romney has so little credibility with conservatives that he continues a compulsive run to the right, leaving independents and moderates in the lurch.

On September 8, 2012, with Pat Robertson looking on approvingly, Romney solemnly promised, "*I will never take God off our coins*". The attenuated inference the voter is supposed to draw is that President Obama likely plans to take God off U.S. coinage. What sparked Romney's sudden burst of Evangelical, monetary piety? One of the elves left the word "God" out of the Democratic platform. That same elf omitted reference to "Jerusalem" as Israel's capital. President Obama, despite the Kenyan anti-colonial tag line, immediately ordered these two omissions restored to the platform language.

A stronger inference that voters may draw, from Mitt's promise to keep God on our coins and in his heart, is that the Romney-Ryan campaign is in desperate straits, flummoxed by evasion of the issues, distortion of their positions and a continual reliance on a series of frantic *Hail Marys* to try to ward off inevitable defeat. It is embarrassing to see Ryan squirm as he tries to twist to the contours of Romney's latest repositioning. Romney criticized the sequestration bill whereby Congress voted for automatic cuts in everything, including defense, if there were no bipartisan agreement on a budget.

Paul Ryan voted for the bill. On September 9, 2012, Ryan denied to Norah O'Donnell three times that he voted in favor of sequestration. Ryan finally sort of admitted that he voted for a process to force the Congress to agree to a budget. Ryan never voted for sequestration, except that is what the law provides—a Treasury holdback of appropriations across the board.

Romney and Ryan have shown themselves to be serial fibbers on abortion, contraception, healthcare, Medicare, Medicaid, the *Path to Prosperity*, sequestration and taxation. On one side, we have the Democrats. On the other side, there are the fibbers and the NFibbers (National Federation of Independent Business), who have convinced small business owners that bankruptcy will overtake them if Obama Care is not repealed.

Intellectual dishonesty is the last refuge of a serial fibber. Mitt Romney will discuss income inequality only in a quiet room, where the poor cannot hear. When asked about his plan to cut tax loopholes, Romney promised that the wealthy would lose some deductions—not saying which ones or whether the Middle Class would be wiped out in the process. When George Stephanopoulos put the same question to Ryan, the V.P. candidate deflected nimbly. Ryan called for a public debate, as if the ABC Network were not public enough. Ryan's other dodge is that, after Romney-Ryan are elected, they will discuss tax and other matters with the Congress—and let the American people know before they have to fill out their tax returns.

With deranged people like Rush Limbaugh cheering Romney-Ryan on, and with multiple *Hail Mary's* falling incomplete, it boggles the mind that forty-seven percent of the electorate believes the Republican claptrap. No wonder Dinesh D'Souza chose America over India. You can sell a bill of goods in the U.S. that Indians would reject outright. Thirty-seven percent of Republicans in Ohio reportedly believe that President Obama was not born in the U.S.

When Mitt Romney hangs around with clowns like Donald Trump, what message does that send to young people in America? Is Romney so insecure that he feels compelled to look for leadership and fund raising in a casino owner who went through four bankruptcies?

Where is Romney's money coming from? Aside from donor bundling by Trump, Romney relies on money from the Koch Brothers and Sheldon Adelson, another casino owner.

A great deal of Romney's money comes through Karl Rove, who escaped indictment in the Valerie Plame Affair after talking his way through *five* Grand Jury appearances. What is the strongest technical plank in Romney's election strategy? Vote suppression. In nine swing-states, Republicans plan to hold power as a minority party by suppressing votes of the majority. Republicans are putting on a civics lesson of how to destroy a democratic Republic.

Laura Ingraham is right, "Shut the party down"—before lasting harm is done to the body politic.

The Romney shambles of the 2012 presidential campaign witnessed the candidate lurch through a never-ending series of *Hail Marys* in a futile attempt to salvage a cratering campaign. Romney's cynical abandonment of the truth is proof positive that Romney is not qualified to hold the office he so desperately seeks.

Romney not only disgraced what is left of his own reputation, but his unscrupulous actions call into question the morality of the Mormon Church. Romney was a bishop and leader in his church. Romney's unprincipled campaign tactics scream that the ends justify the means in Romney's Mormon way of life.

Romney is behind in polls in Florida, Ohio and Virginia. Romney's stellar performance in the first debate with the President tightened the race considerably. If President Obama continues to hold but two of these three states, Romney's loss is a virtual certainty. In a reckless attempt to ward off what looks like an inevitable defeat, Romney decided to abandon his integrity.

Romney joins the chorus of dishonest voices calling our President an alien who does not appreciate or even understand American values. Romney adopted the *Big Lie* that our President apologized to the rioters instead of protecting the right of an ex-convict to disseminate a toxic libel of Islam that sparked riots in twenty countries and resulted in the death of Ambassador Christopher Stevens and three other consulate officers in Benghazi, Libya, on 9/11/12.

Romney's major chance to win on 11/6/12 is dependent upon the *Big Lie* and vote suppression sponsored by Republican-controlled legislatures or Republican Secretaries of State in nine swing states. The right to vote of millions of U.S. citizens is subject to the outcome of more than a half dozen law suits pending in state and federal courts.

Romney is an amoral robot, inevitably programmed to do whatever appears expedient to win, and whose defeat will spell the beginning of the end for a political party that no longer has any concept of truth, liberty or justice. Our nation is not going to elect a weathervane. The G.O.P. has not changed for the better over the past forty years. The unbroken line of dirty political tricks remains uninterrupted from Richard Nixon, Doug Chapin, Donald Segretti and his understudy, a young Karl Rove, right up to the present Republican establishment that started to delegitimize our President before Inauguration Day.

Republican dirty tricks have gone from amateur hour under Donald Segretti and apprentice Karl Rove to professional emasculating of the 14th Amendment under Republican Secretaries of State and Republican-controlled legislatures, who collectively pursue the strategy of Vote Suppression and Voter Intimidation. Why try to sabotage your opponent's campaign, when you can strike at the heart of the matter simply by undercounting the votes of your opponent's supporters?

Some ingenious Republicans have pushed the fight to an even earlier point in the brawl. States, to a great extent, control voting as a matter of historical precedent. Why not try to keep President Obama's name off the ballot? The beauty of this devious device is that Republicans would not have to worry about Vote Suppression in states where the President is not on the ballot.

As strange as this sounds (treating our President as an undocumented alien), there are always Republican extremists eager to accommodate any loopy conservative ploy to lever the President out of office. On 5/18/12, Arizona Secretary of State Ken Bennett gave a radio interview saying that he was waiting for the State of Hawaii to confirm that President Obama was born there. Bennett, of course, later made it clear that he is not a "birther". An Arizona citizen (presumably identified to Bennett as such) made the request. Bennett is not asking Michigan for Mitt Romney's birth certificate because no one made that request. This is irrefutable proof that the number of loopy Republicans in Arizona is exponentially greater than the number of loopy Democrats in Arizona.

On 9/13/12, Kris Kobach, Secretary of the State of Kansas, met as a member of the Kansas Objections Board to determine if President Obama is eligible to be on the ballot in Kansas. Kobach continued the matter until he could obtain proof from Hawaii of Obama's U.S. birth. The Kansas Objections Board did not act spontaneously. There was a complainant, who just wanted to make certain that the President is not an undocumented alien. Of course, Kris Kobach is not a "birther", either. Rumor has it that the objector withdrew the complaint to avoid the glare of controversy.

Kobach is a hardliner on immigration. Kobach was instrumental in drafting Arizona's immigration law, SB 1070, which Governor Jan Brewer (R-AZ) recently signed as the *"Papers, Please"* law. Kobach seems to yearn for exposure in Arizona, where he is co-chair of Mitt Romney's campaign. Kobach is an advisor to Romney on, you guessed it, immigration policy. The contours of the Republican Platform on immigration took shape in part from input from Kobach. Hispanics, like other demographic groups, somehow get the feeling that Republicans do not appreciate them.

Ann Romney pandered to one demographic at the Republican Convention by exclaiming, "I love you women". Mitt Romney appeared on Univision, but no one believed him when he tried to be a friend of Hispanics. Mitt's anti-immigrant stance is cast in concrete.

***

"The Budget Control Act represents a victory for those committed to controlling spending and growing our economy."
Paul Ryan.

Chapter -4-
Budget Control Act

Paul Ryan sat on the Super Committee of Congress and vigorously supported sequestration as part of the Budget Control Act of 2011. Ryan voted against the Simpson-Bowles proposal to achieve fiscal integrity, and then criticized President Obama for not adopting the Simpson-Bowles Report of the Super Committee.

In a misguided attempt to weaken President Obama, Republicans refused to agree to an increase in the National Debt. The money was already spent or committed, but Republicans would not sign on to an increase in the Debt. The net result was a downgrade of America's debt, the first downgrade in 230 years. The Budget Control Act was a stopgap measure to deal with the fiscal crisis.

Sequestration (lovingly referred to as going over the fiscal cliff) is a device enacted by Congress to cut all Departments and programs across the board by $1.2 trillion over ten years if there is not bipartisan agreement on a budget by December 31, 2012. The cuts generally range from 8-10%. After the election on November 6, 2012, the first major battle will be over the budget.

If the Democrats take back the House and maintain control of the Senate, the battle will change dramatically. Even though newly elected members of Congress will not be seated until January 2013, Republicans may come to their senses if they lose large in November. After all, the Tea Party extremists feel they are doing what the electorate mandated in the 2010 election.

Mitt Romney feels that the sequestration provision of the Budget Control Act was not a good idea. This causes Paul Ryan to squirm a bit. Ryan claims he did not vote technically for sequestration. Ryan merely voted for the Budget Control Act as a means of forcing the parties to agree to a budget.

Ryan also boasts that the Romney-Ryan team will repeal Obama Care in its entirety. Romney, however, as an accurate weathervane, now claims that he will keep the better features of Obama Care, which, coincidentally, are identical to that unspeakable subject— Romney Care. Romney cannot praise Romney Care because

Conservatives loathe Obama Care. The Conservative Universe presents a tortured image of the real world. It is as if the inmates have taken over the asylum.

Republicans have moved so far to the extreme right that Rush Limbaugh and Ann Coulter are centrists in the new Conservative galaxy.

***

"Hateful to me as the gates of Hades is that man who hides one thing in his heart and speaks another."

Homer.

Chapter -5-

Most Deceptive Campaign.

Marketing is convincing consumers to buy something, whether needed or not. Advertising is the means to effect marketing. Political advertising often seeks to sell something disguised as something else. Republican candidates are especially prone to use false advertising because Republicans represent the upper two percent. The ninety-eight percent ordinarily would not be easily persuaded to vote for policies that favor the Koch Brothers and Sheldon Adelson.

Republicans have a remedy to dissuade the electorate from voting for Middle Class interests. First, it is necessary to smear the

Democratic candidate as someone who does not stand for American values. Republicans have a conference called the Values Voter Summit. A Values Voter can choose the Republican candidate, even where the Republican candidate plans to make Medicare a Voucher Program and to privatize Social Security.

Public policy issues do not control the Values Voter. Nor do realities. That is why the Romney campaign stated that they will not be limited by fact-checkers. Romney is selling sham all-American feelings that are untethered from bothersome facts. Visceral trumps cerebral in the G.O.P. universe by using social wedge issues to divide.

The Republican Convention was a study in how to make it appear that things are not as they seem. Not enough minority delegates in the Little Tent party? Seat the delegates from the District of Columbia and the territories front and center. Behind in the women vote? Have Ann Romney declare, "I love you women!" Need to keep angry white men angry with government. Have Clint Eastwood debate an empty chair in lieu of the President.

Want to appear tough? Put on Governor Chris Christie (R-NJ) at the Convention. It was jarring, however, to see the hard sell of Christie follow soon after the soft sell of Ann Romney. Christy was selling himself for 2016, more than he was selling Romney for 2012.

Republicans are a sorry paradigm for what a political party should be. In the broadest sense, Republicans and Mitt Romney deserve each other. Neither has a core built around principle. Each has a pragmatic desire to hold power at all costs. Each is a master of the *Big Lie*. Each is selling feelings and not issues based on facts.

Romney announced that he would adopt the *Big Lie* strategy. Ironically, he did this by asserting that President Obama is not truthful. Romney claims that he will reduce tax rates for all taxpayers. Romney claims that he will generate revenue by eliminating tax loopholes for upper income taxpayers. When pressed for details, Romney retreats to vague generalities. Romney knows that if he mentions eliminating deductions for mortgage interest or state and local taxes, it will be the Middle Class who will bear the brunt more than the upper two percent.

Paul Ryan freely admits that the Romney-Ryan team will discuss taxes with Congress after the election. Until then, the electorate will be kept in the dark.

***

"The human brain is a complex organ with the wonderful power of enabling man to find reasons for continuing to believe whatever it is he wants to believe."

Voltaire.

Chapter -6-

G.O.P. Delusion.

Republicans are an endangered species because they believe their own propaganda. A majority of the electorate, however, does not. The *Big Lie* is effective precisely because it is so colossal that people cannot believe it could be false. "Birthers" raised doubts about President Obama's birth in Hawaii. When the "birther" lie collapsed, Republican credibility fell with it. Leverage on the *Big Lie* is as strong on the way down as it is on the way up.

Republicans cannot separate themselves from the "birthers". Republican Secretaries of State in Arizona and Kansas questioned whether President Obama should be on the ballot on November 6, 2012. When Ken Bennett and Kris Kobach meekly dropped their cynical gesture to the "birthers", Republican credibility went down another notch. When Mitt Romney told the crowd on 8/21/12 that "No one's ever asked to see my birth certificate", Republican credibility continued the downward spiral. Romney says he was joking, but the partisan crowd cheered.

"*I don't care what Fact Check says*", objects Peter King (R-NY) to Soledad O'Brien on 9/17/12. King is Chair of House Homeland Security. King is a leader in the Republican smear of President Obama. King claims that Barack Obama made an Apology Tour of the Middle East in 2009. King voted for the Wall St. Bailout under George W. Bush in 2008 and against the Stimulus and *Lilly Ledbetter Fair Pay Act* under President Obama in 2009.

King claims that the mobs in the Middle East are there because of perceived weakness of President Obama. King was silent when mobs ran amok under George W. Bush. Nor does King blame President Bush for the attack on 9/11/01. King can enjoy a delusion as much as Dinesh D'Souza. The House of Reprehensibles will continue its path of smear and fear until the voters take back America. When Nancy Pelosi takes back the Speaker's gavel, King will no longer have the Chair of Homeland Security to give credence to the *Big Lie* about President Obama's leadership.

***

"Why is propaganda so much more successful when it stirs up hatred than when it tries to stir up friendly feeling?"
Bertrand Russell.

Chapter -7-

Propaganda.

At the heart of the Republican plan to lever President Obama out of office is a propaganda campaign to delegitimize the President as not one of us. The word "foreign" is used to describe the President. As the facts come out, however, Mitt Romney and John Sununu look foreign. It is simply un-American to tell fibs about people. The *Big Lie* implodes as the bona fides of the fibbers comes into question.

Romney shipped jobs to China and India. Romney has an equity interest in a dozen Bain Capital ventures in the Cayman Islands. Romney kept money in a Swiss Bank Account and in other off-shore locations. Romney's reputation as a manager is in tatters after the wheels came off his 2012 campaign.

Conservative writers eagerly seek to block the advance of progressive ideas. Many of the books currently offered by the Right Wing are irrational polemics against Barack Obama, such as:

Obama's America, Unmaking the American Dream—another delusion by Dinesh D'Souza;

No Higher Power, Obama's War On religious Freedom, by Phyllis Schlafly and George Neumayr, a screed touted as Obama "working to create one nation under him rather than one nation under God";

Obama: The Great Destroyer, by David Limbaugh, who claims that Obama is "knocking down the free market economy";

Defending the Free Market by Robert A. Sirico, who claims that capitalism protects human dignity; and

The Amateur by Edward Klein, who claims, 'It's amateur hour in the White House'.

Other publishers are aware of President Obama as a treasure trove of book deals. One book, however, sums up the anti-Obama hysteria. *The Manchurian President: Barack Obama's Ties to Communists, Socialists and other American Extremists*, by Aaron Klein and Brenda J. Elliott, published by World Net Daily Books.

Romney has taken so many positions that he has lost all credibility in the propaganda war. Politicians usually try to tell their audiences what the spectators want to hear. With the advent of videotape, however, the continual fibbing over time will erode a candidate's integrity. When Romney took flak in September for writing off half the Nation as moochers in a fund raiser in May 2012, Romney immediately corrected. Romney told an Hispanic audience on Univision Network on 9/20/12 that he is the candidate of 100% of the people. Romney promised not to deport twelve million undocumented workers. Pulling out all the stops, Romney admitted being the grandfather of Obamacare. Conservative Obama haters are getting panicky.

At this point, Romney's campaign came off the rails. Co-Chair Tim Pawlenty, former Governor of Minnesota, resigned to take a position as a lobbyist for the banking industry. Peggy Noonan, former speech writer for Ronald Reagan, called Romney's campaign "incompetent", "in need of intervention" and "a rolling calamity". It is too late, however, for Romney to recalibrate. Everyone remembers Ted Kennedy's tease from the 1994 Senate Race. "I am pro-choice. My Opponent is multiple choice."

In a frantic attempt to change the topic of Romney's disdain for half of America as government dependent, Republicans dredged up a fourteen-year old video of Barack Obama as an Illinois State Senator in 1998, speaking the buzz word "redistribution". Obama went on to praise competiveness, but the Republicans do not show that segment of the Obama discourse. By tying Obama to redistribution, Republicans desperately want to tag Obama as a Socialist or a Communist. Every tax in history, however, has a redistributive aspect. The electorate is rejecting the Republican *Big Lie*. Obama represents the American Middle Class. Mitt Romney and John Sununu do not.

***

"It's disgraceful that the Obama Administration's first response was not to condemn attacks on our diplomatic missions, but to sympathize with those who waged the attacks."
Mitt Romney, September 12, 2012

Chapter -8-
Deconstructing Mitt Romney

By seeking to make political capital out of a national tragedy, the killing of our Ambassador in Libya, Romney demonstrated either a callous disregard for propriety or an inability to think clearly in a fast moving situation. Some fool in Los Angeles made a Moslem-baiting movie that defamed the Prophet Mohammad. The movie made it to U-Tube in July 2012. A Moslem cleric incited his flock in Cairo in September. The American Embassy put out a statement that it would be prudent not to offend the religion of others.

That evening Romney complained that America was apologizing for its values. Despite the First Amendment, is it an "American value" to disseminate a movie that defames a religion? On September 11, 2012, crowds demonstrated at the U.S. Embassy in Cairo. In an unrelated act of planned terrorism the same day, an armed group, that may be affiliated with al Qaeda in North Africa, attacked the Consulate in Benghazi, Libya with rocket-propelled grenades, setting fire to the Consulate and killing the American Ambassador, Christopher Stevens, and three other consular officials.

Five days later, U.S. Ambassador to the U.N. appeared on the Sunday Talk Shows and described the Benghazi attack as growing out of a demonstration against the anti-Moslem movie. John McCain and Lindsey Graham, later joined by Kelly Ayotte and Susan Collins, pilloried Rice for not labeling the Benghazi attack as terrorism. Rice's choice of words cost her the nomination as Secretary of State.

Romney doubled down on his initial complaint about apologizing for American values. No one apologized for American values. The Cairo Embassy saw a potentially dangerous demonstration coming and attempted to defuse the situation by suggesting that it is imprudent to defame a religion.

Romney is so desperate to cast our President as "foreign", as not one of us and as apologetic for American values that Romney invented an apology that was never made and attributed the non-existent apology to the President. Romney demonstrated once again that he is not qualified to lead the Nation. Romney's 2012 campaign is a never-ending series of *Hail Marys* that collectively amount to a shambles.

The trip to the London Olympics was a public relations disaster. When asked how he thought the Brits would manage, Romney could not restrain from being the superior manager since he managed the Salt Lake City Winter Olympics in 2002. Romney offered that the security situation in London was disconcerting. British Prime Minister David Cameron reminded the world that it is easier to manage an Olympics in the middle of nowhere, a biting reference to Salt Lake City.

Boris Johnson, the Mayor of London, mocked Romney's critique of British management. "There's a guy called Mitt Romney who wants to know whether we're ready. Are we ready? Are we ready? Yes, we are!"

Romney had to skedaddle from the Olympic games before people might associate him with Ann Romney's dancing horse, Refalca. Romney traipsed off to Israel to try to undermine the President with

Romney's former associate Prime Minister Benjamin Netanyahu. Conventional wisdom is that Romney's trip sought to win over the American Jewish vote. Romney's real target is the Evangelicals, who love Israelis for the role they will play in the *End Times* set piece. The Israelis are necessary as a backdrop to the *Rapture of the Evangelicals*, who will be swept to paradise. The Israelis will be *Left Behind* with the Arabs. The American Jewish community likely will support President Obama despite Netanyahu's histrionics about war with Iran.

The last stop on Romney's international sojourn was Warsaw. Why Poland? There are a dozen cities in the American mid-west with large Polish populations. Poland is nominally a Catholic country. The Catholic strategy was already taking form. Romney's selection of Paul Ryan was another *Hail Mary* calculated to advance the Catholic strategy. Ryan's planned raid on Medicaid, however, is contrary to Catholic social teaching, as are additional tax cuts for the upper two percent.

Conventional wisdom laments the failure of President Obama to get along with Prime Minister Netanyahu on a personal level. This is another D'Souza-type delusion. The friction has nothing to do with personalities. Netanyahu thought that it was time to attack Iran to prevent acquisition of nuclear weaponry. Netanyahu decided that the U.S. must lead the attack on Iran, and must launch hostilities now. Obama is understandably not enthusiastic about starting another war after a ten-year *Fiasco* in Iraq and a likely thirteen-year bottomless pit in Afghanistan.

Obama's reluctance to meet with Netanyahu to plan a war against Iran did not stop the Israeli Prime Minister. Netanyahu appeared on the U.S. Sunday talk shows to whip up war against Iran. This is unprecedented in the annals of American history. Needless to say, Romney is delighted at any embarrassment to the Obama Administration.

Obama's refusal to jump into war against Iran at the snap of Netanyahu's fingers is not anti-Israeli. In response to Netanyahu's posturing against President Obama, one of the Israeli opposition leaders asked, "Which government do you want to remove first, Iran's or America's". Obama's reluctance to meet with Netanyahu near the time of the world's U.N. Assembly addresses is eminently understandable in view of Netanyahu's intention to press publicly for the U.S. to attack Iran.

One policy fact is paramount. America, and not Israel, will dictate what wars America should fight, when, where and with which allies alongside. President Obama should not have to explain this fundamental truth to Netanyahu. Israel's insecurity is understandable. Netanyahu's attempt to force America's hand is intolerable. Romney's taking advice from neocons in this matter is all the more frightening in view of the neocon-led war George W. Bush fought in

Iraq. Seventeen of twenty-four Romney Advisors are left-overs from the Bush Administration.

While campaigning on 9/12/12 in Florida, where the American Jewish vote is important, Romney said he could not imagine that as President he would ever refuse to meet with the Prime Minister of Israel. Chalk one up for the neocons. Romney's phony patriotism shone through. The problem Romney has is that his reputation, at least in politics, is that he is a serial fibber. Romney will say whatever he thinks is expedient to win.

Romney writes off the forty-seven percent

In May 2012, Romney appeared at a private, $50,000 a plate, fundraiser in Boca Raton, FL, to stroke some wealthy donors. Someone secretly videotaped Romney's presentation that frankly wrote off forty-seven percent of the electorate as dependent on government assistance and not amenable to Romney's tax cut message. "My job is not to worry about those people. I'll never convince them they should take personal responsibility and care for their lives." This was the real Romney speaking to wealthy donors. No pretense about representing all the people.

As we witness the Romney shambles in the frantic, disjointed trip to London, Israel and Poland—Romney's compulsive kowtowing to the conservative base through the selection of Paul Ryan as V.P. and the advocacy of extreme positions on contraception, immigration, defense, Medicare, health care and taxation—there is a realization that the Middle Class American in the race is Barack Obama. The foreigner is Mitt Romney, who stashes his cash offshore in any event. Romney even wants to outsource to Israel the right to declare America at war.

How many *Hail Marys*, to stave off disaster, is one candidate entitled to?

***

"If you can't beat Obama with this record, then shut down the party." Laura Ingraham, September 10, 2012

Chapter 9

The Party's Over.

When it becomes more apparent that Barack Obama will prevail on November 6, 2012, conservatives will abandon Romney in droves. After all, Mitt is not their man. This was a marriage of convenience, not a love story. Laura Ingraham claims that 2012 is a "gimme election". All Romney has to do is to answer 'present'. Oh, yes, Romney should also stop fibbing and putting his foot in his mouth. Laura assumes that most people will conclude that they are not better off now than they were four years ago. This assumption is nothing short of a D'Souza delusion.

In 2008, there was a financial panic that wiped out the U.S. commercial paper market (on which major corporations depended for short-term liquidity) and threatened the existence of the American banking system. The stock market headed for 650 on the Dow. Merrill Lynch and Countrywide Home Loans had to be rescued by Bank of America, which was financially stressed by the rescue. J.P. Morgan acquired Bear Stearns. Wells Fargo bought Wachovia. The U.S. Housing Industry collapsed from coast to coast. The auto industry lacked cash to operate, except for Ford Motor Company. The U.S. Treasury took over mortgage giants Fannie Mae and Freddie Mac

If General Motors and Chrysler liquidated, the auto parts supply chain likely would go bankrupt, taking Ford down with them. Lehman Brothers, which persisted since the 1850s, was insolvent, and, after desperately looking in vain for a partner with cash, filed bankruptcy when the Bush Administration turned a cold shoulder. AIG was *Too Big to Fail*, and required $85 billion from the U.S. government to stay afloat.

Secretary of the Treasury Henry Paulson and George W. Bush convinced the Congress to fund TARP (Troubled Asset Relief Program) with $700 billion to keep the doors of the nation's banks open. Millions of mortgagors were in default. The wheels of commerce ground to a screeching halt for lack of the lubricant that is money. Initially TARP intended to allow banks to purchase toxic assets to relieve the default crisis. TARP soon evolved to a loan program to hundreds of banks to help shore up their capital structure. The banks survived, but stopped making loans. Mortgagors were stuck with billions in toxic loans and assets with no equity.

Companies reacted swiftly to the financial panic by laying off millions of employees. This created a downward spiral, where lack of demand for goods and services caused more layoffs of employees. It soon became apparent that the Wall Street Investment banks could not survive as pure (using the term loosely) investment banks. All of the investment banks were allowed to adopt new charters that allowed them to become depositary institutions as well, thereby opening the Federal Reserve Discount window for Wall Street Banks to access millions in cash.

Mitt Romney's remedy for the auto industry was encapsulated in his 11/18/08 *Op-Ed* in the New York Times, "*Let Detroit Go Bankrupt*". Fortunately, President Barack Obama had the good sense to lend billions to Chrysler and General Motors, and saved a million jobs. If Ohio and a number of other manufacturing states support President Obama on November 6, 2012, it will be in no small part because of the President's heroic rescue of the auto industry. If Laura Ingraham thinks that 2008 was a great year, she is qualified to attend an economic seminar delivered by Dinesh D'Souza.

"A Final Hail Mary"

After many fits and starts in his campaign, Romney determined in mid-September to outline how he would govern. According to the

AP, "Romney will seek this week to explain more what he would do as President, a strategy shift intended to change the trajectory of a race that President Barack Obama appears to be winning". Romney will dazzle the voters with "a new batch of TV ads".

Romney's problem, however, is that a wide swath of independents, moderate Republicans and Democrats are skeptical of Romney's ability to tell the truth. The one additional tax return Romney promised turned out to be a manipulation of the tax rate Romney paid. Romney represented that he never paid less than 13% tax. For 2011, Romney intentionally understated deductions to keep his tax rate above 14%. Romney can recover his tax overpayment at any time by filing an amended return after the election. Where are the details of the tax policy Romney promotes?

Romney manipulates facts to suit his purposes. When his needs change, and verifiable facts are inconsistent with his changed circumstances, Romney changes the facts retroactively. Romney wanted and received a deduction for his Utah home while he managed the 2002 Winter Olympics in Salt Lake City. Romney filed taxes in Utah as a resident of Utah in order to qualify for the homestead deduction.

While running for Governor of Massachusetts later in 2002, Romney was required to show that he was a resident of the state for seven years. Romney represented to the people of Massachusetts that he filed Massachusetts taxes as a resident of Massachusetts for the time he was living in Utah. When that turned out to be a colossal fib, Romney changed the facts by retroactively filing amended tax returns with Utah and Massachusetts to claim residency in the Bay State.

By the wave of a magic wand, Romney claims he will create twelve million new jobs if elected President. If conservatives do not trust Romney, however, why should independents, moderates and progressives? Paul Ryan will work the fiscal issues, but he has no credibility as well.

***

"Birds of a feather flock together."

Anonymous.

Chapter -10-

Down Ticket Blues.

In the case of Mitt Romney, a wide variety of conservative birds distanced themselves from the top of the ticket. During the 2012 Republican Primary, the most consistent theme from the aspirants was, 'I am not Mitt Romney'. At a $50,000 plate fundraiser in May, Romney famously portrayed 47% of the American people as moochers. As word of Romney's disdain for nearly half of America spread, Republican candidates for Congress suddenly developed Romney-phobia.

Tommy Thompson, hoping to represent the people of Wisconsin in the U.S. Senate against Democratic candidate, U.S. Rep. Tammy Baldwin , noted that the top of the ticket may adversely affect down ticket candidates. Linda McMahon, maven of world wrestling promotions and Senate hopeful in Connecticut against Democratic incumbent Richard Blumenthal, expressed a view different from Romney's. The same was true of former Governor Linda Lingle, running against Mazie Hirono to be the Senator from Hawaii.

Scott Brown, incumbent Senator from Massachusetts, in a tough race with Elizabeth Warren, disavowed Romney's scorn of half of the population. Brown was supposed to debate Warren in the evening of 9/20/12. Brown flew to Washington that day to be available for important Senate votes. Senate Majority Leader Harry Reid canceled all further Senate votes for the day, thereby forcing Brown to return to Boston for the debate with Warren.

Brown's foremost point in the debate was his opening challenge that Warren pretended to be part Cherokee Indian. Warren calmly replied that she believed the ancestral stories told to her by her mother, her father and her aunts and uncles, and did not ask her mother for documentary proof. Brown came across as the weakest contender for the Massachusetts Senate Seat in the past two hundred years. Brown voted against President Obama's jobs bills on three occasions, allegedly to save voters a tax increase. Brown continually referred to his opponent as "Professor" Warren as if the teacher tag would increase Brown's chances of winning.

Massachusetts voters know Mitt Romney well from Romney's time as Governor. Barack Obama leads Romney by double digits in the Bay State. Elizabeth Warren should beat Scott Brown on her own merits. By the way, Brown has nothing against American Indians. Brown contends that Warren received unfair preferences in admission to college and appointment to jobs as result of claims of having a native American heritage. Brown demands that Warren produce documentary evidence from college admissions offices and employers to refute Brown's accusation.

Brown's paid staffers appeared at a rally, yelling war chants and giving tomahawk chops to demean Warren's heritage. The Chief of the Cherokee Nation, Bill John Baker demanded an apology for racist behavior of Brown's staffers. Brown demonstrated one immutable fact. Brown truly belongs in the grotesquely misshapen Republican Party of 2012. Ted Kennedy may rest easy.

***

"The agent for the destruction of Medicare was chosen as V.P." House Leader Nancy Pelosi to Rachel Maddow on September 26, 2012.

Chapter -11-

What Happens in 2016.

One of the best things that could happen in 2016 is that the Koch Brothers and Sheldon Adelson may refuse to write Republicans a blank check, with which to undermine the American electoral process. The Nation would be a better place if Karl Rove were not given hundreds of millions of dollars to purchase anti-American propaganda ads. It is obvious that the election system is broken. As presently applied by the U.S. Supreme Court, the First Amendment equates money with free speech.

The question is not whether there will be Republican candidates eager to run for president in 2016. Chris Christie, Jeb Bush and a score of other hopefuls will be ready to jump in. The Koch Brothers may enter Herman Cain in the contest. The question is whether there will be a Republican Party in existence in 2016. If Republicans lose in 2012, it may call into question the viability of the Republican Party in its present form.

Ironically, the Values Voter Summit Party, demonstrated that it is "foreign" to the American way of life. Republicans spent four years smearing President Obama as not one of us. Conservatives demanded to see the President's birth certificate. The certificate of live birth was not good enough. "Birthers" demanded to see the long-form birth certificate. Of course, die-hards claimed the long-form certificate presented was a forgery.

Donald Trump became the drum major of the Birther Brigade. All the while, Mitt Romney said nothing, except to note that Barack Obama's ideas were foreign. Romney trotted out John Sununu, who long ago became a naturalized citizen, to wish that Barack Obama would "learn to be an American".

Finally, Mitt Romney spoke out. "No one ever asked me for my birth certificate." No one doubts where Romney was born. The only doubt is whether Romney represents American Values. A review of the facts shows that Romney is a pathological fibber, who is not Middle Class in any sense of the word.

Romney craves to be the self-made man. Romney claims he did not inherit his wealth. There was a million dollar gift from his father that the son gave to charity. Ann Romney, however, recalls how they went through Mitt's college years without working. Ann remembers Mitt periodically selling shares of stock, a gift from his father, to cover living expenses during Mitt's college years.

Then there is the myth of Mitt the Corporate Manager. Romney never managed a manufacturing company. Mitt headed up a corporate raider that used the assets of target companies to finance leveraged buy-outs. Some of the companies Mitt raided survived. Other went through the Bain Capital chop shop and saw employees' jobs outsourced to China and India. Mitt Romney has no clue how to create jobs, except in China and India.

Romney is the All-American, who keeps his treasure in Switzerland and the Cayman Islands. There are two major skills that Romney possesses. One is fibbing. The other is paying as little income tax as possible. For 2011, however, Romney overpaid his taxes by understating his deductions. Romney manipulated his taxes to make sure he paid more than 13% tax, part of which he can recover by filing an amended return. In Romney world, Romney makes up the facts.

If the Republican Party still exists in 2016, the Electorate must inspect the candidates carefully. All this talk about Jeb Bush being a kinder, gentler version of brother George is nothing but claptrap. Jeb already established himself as a fibber. At the 2012 Republican Convention, Jeb proudly proclaimed that George W. Bush "kept us safe". May be 9/11/01 was Bill Clinton's fault?

Jeb Bush talks about giving parents choices and vouchers to allow placement of children in schools out of the neighborhood. Jeb Bush uses the analogy of the supermarket. When you come to the milk section, you can choose, regular milk, chocolate milk, strawberry milk, etc. Why not let the parents choose a charter school. It may be dangerous to fund an exodus from inner city schools, if left behind is a decaying shell of a public school system. Beware the Republican strategy to privatize everything, including the schools and the jails.

The Republican Party is the greatest threat to the American way of life.

Does Jeb Bush favor making Medicare a voucher program? As long as Jeb Bush is a Republican, the Electorate must assume that Jeb Bush favors Republican policies. Will Jeb Bush be a captive of the Evangelicals and the Neoconservatives? When Jeb Bush and Chris Christie are trotted out in 2016, let the buyer beware.

***

"Government of the people, by the people and for the people shall not perish from the earth."
Abraham Lincoln, finale of the Gettysburg Address.

Chapter -12-

What Happened in 2012?

The failure of Mitt Romney to gain traction with a majority of the American Electorate is the result of many factors. What is surprising is that Romney managed to hold in for a while at 47-49% in the polls. A more deceitful Republican candidate may have won. Herman Cain claims he would do better because his ideas are more profound than Romney's. Fooling a greater number of voters, however, is an empty accomplishment. Republican propaganda can only go so far. The nearly four-year campaign to delegitimize President Obama was destined to fail. The *Big Lie* is like a balloon that bursts when jabbed with the truth.

What if Romney won?

If Romney were to win the election by three percentage points, the Nation would have reluctantly accepted the inevitable. If Romney won by only 500,000 votes spread over nine swing states, the reaction would have been toxic. There would be cries of another stolen election, whether the Supreme Court chimed in or not in 2012. The fact that nine swing states, controlled by the Republicans or having Republican Secretaries of State, actively sought to suppress Democratic votes would have raised the issue of Romney's illegitimacy. The Nation is not ready for another stolen election, as happened in 2000.

There is no doubt but that Romney is a failure as a presidential candidate. The Nation does not want to vote for a weathervane. Romney's inability to manage is demonstrated by his inability to manage his own campaign, which lurched from one extreme to another. In private, Romney wants to represent only 53% of the people, having written off 47% as moochers. The math is unworkable unless Romney could take 95% of the 53%. Romney is strongly in favor of cracking down on undocumented workers, but only when Romney speaks to the conservative base.

When speaking to Hispanics, however, Romney pretends to be their friend. To impress the conservative base during the primary, Romney promised to repeal Obamacare the first day in office. In September, Romney moderated and said he would keep the best features of Obama care. Romney then conceded that he might even be the grandfather of Obamacare. If the conservatives suddenly embraced Obamacare, however, Romney would go along like a puppy.

What is inexplicable is the failure of the Republicans to have any discussion, rational or irrational, of the *Affordable Care Act* ("ACA"*)*. Because the Republicans take an inflexible stance on health care, Romney is forced to ape the unreasonable posture of the conservatives. The fibbers and the NFIBbers (Nat'l Fed. Ind. Bus.) compulsively want to repeal the ACA out of reflex loathing of President Obama.

The contorted position of Republicans leads to a bizarre result. Romney cannot talk about a health care regime that he helped to install successfully in Massachusetts. The Nation's first national health care system (Obamacare) is a taboo subject for conservatives. Instead of cooperating to find a way to control costs, Republicans vow only to repeal the ACA. Indeed, the House of Reprehensibles passed 31 separate bills in 2010-2012 to repeal, defund or otherwise cripple the ACA.

The stalemate in Congress is not the result of President Obama failing to work with conservatives. It appears that conservatives realize that the Republican Party is no longer viable. Barack Obama demonstrated that Republican policies are calculated to flow money and power to the upper two percent. Since the 98% are reluctant to embrace poverty to empower the rich, the Republican reaction is to try to destroy President Obama. "Out, out, damned spot!"

Republicans accuse President Obama of dividing the people against one another. Class warfare is the battle cry. It is Romney and the Republicans, however, who are waging class warfare. Republicans have used class division to divide and conquer for years. Using Evangelicals as a bludgeon, Republicans tried to destroy any candidate who favored Women's Reproductive Rights.

The marriage of the Republican Party with Evangelicals is an unholy alliance. The result is a dangerous combination of religion and politics. It may be a valid policy issue to try to reduce the number of abortions. The problem arises when Evangelicals push to criminalize abortions. Reprehensible Todd Akin (R-MO) made the mistake of referring to the junk science that some Evangelicals rely upon to insinuate their beliefs into government programs.

Akin infamously stated that if there is a "legitimate rape", women "can shut their bodies down". In other words, women cannot become pregnant from forcible rape according to junk science. Evangelicals want to punish raped women a second time by denying contraceptive services.

Republican Party leaders, except for Tony Perkins of the Family Research Council and perennial Evangelical Mike Huckabee, dropped Akin like a bad habit. Karl Rove cut off funding for Akin from Rove's Super PACs. Senator Claire McCaskill (D-MO) took a lead in the race against Reprehensible Akin.

Shunning one errant Republican for relying on junk science to deny Women's Reproductive Rights, however, is not enough to salvage a moribund Republican Party. The Founders gave us a democratic Republic, in which the People elect their government. The People are rejecting the *Big Lie* of the *Little Tent* Republican Party.

In late September, Akin could no longer be replaced on the ballot. In a disgusting show of cynicism, Republicans and Republican money are creeping back to the Akin campaign. The creepiest is Newt Gingrich, who is desperate to be relevant to something, somewhere, somehow.

Despite $800 million in propaganda ads, the Republican Party is going down in flames. Propaganda will not help. Vote Suppression will not help. The fibbers and the NFIBbers cannot help the anti-everyone party. Republicans are anti-democratic, anti-Affordable Care Act, anti-intellectual, anti-science, anti-environmental protection, anti-Women's Reproductive Rights, anti-immigrant, anti-labor, anti-union, anti-global warming, anti-poor, anti-Middle Class, antigovernment, anti-tax and mindlessly anti-everything President Obama endorses.

The Republican Party lacks a valid secular purpose to exist. It is not enough to protect the billions of Sheldon Adelson and the Koch Brothers. The Republican Party has no guiding principle to sustain it. Small government has a ring to it. It is a tinny sound, however, when there is realization that small government is necessary only to ensure lower taxes for the upper two percent. Mitt Romney wants to help the poor but he wants to defund many of the programs that would help the poor. Paul Ryan became a fiscal hawk only after George W. Bush left office. Ryan plans to cut Medicaid to fund a tax cut for the rich. On 9/21/12, an AARP audience booed and jeered Ryan as he tried to sell repeal of the *Affordable Care Act.*

Republicans fail to appreciate the universality of the Democratic Party. There were Mexicans living legally in Arizona before Governor Jan Brewer's ancestors got off the boat. Now, Brewer demands, 'Papers, please!'.

Republicans ran a campaign of innuendo, smear and fear against President Obama. After a series of failed *Hail Marys*, Romney decided to get into the gutter. Newt Gingrich, Donald Trump, Paul Ryan and John Sununu happily joined. The American People, however, will have none of it. The Republican Party is finished. The Electorate no longer believes Rush Limbaugh, Ann Coulter, David Limbaugh and the rest of the extremists. The most dangerous

Republican, however, is Jeb Bush, who will try to emerge in 2016 as a moderate—with enticing, destructive vouchers in hand. Beware the vouchers! There is no such animal as a moderate Republican.

***

www.ingramcontent.com/pod-product-compliance
Lightning Source LLC
Chambersburg PA
CBHW060004300526
45794CB00003B/1078